Animals in Danger!

Written by Ellen Catala

Illustrated by Ka Botzis

Troll

Copyright © 1999 by Troll Communications L.L.C.

Planet Reader is an imprint of Troll Communications L.L.C.

Printed in the United States of America.   0-8167-6337-2

10 9 8 7 6 5 4 3 2 1

Welcome to Planet Reader!

Invite your child on a journey to a wonderful, imaginative place—
the limitless universe of reading! And there's no better traveling
companion than you, the parent. Every time you and your child read
together you send out an important message: Reading can be rewarding
and *fun*. This understanding is essential to helping your child build the
skills and confidence he or she needs as an emerging reader.

Here are some tips for sharing Planet Reader stories with your child:

Be open! Some children like to listen to or read the whole story and
then ask questions. Some children will stop on every page with a
question or a comment. Either way is fine; the most important thing
is that your child feels reading is a pleasurable experience.

Be understanding! Sometimes your child might need a direct answer.
If he or she points to a word and asks you to tell what it is, do so.
Other times, your child may want to sound out a word or stop to figure
out a sentence independently. Allow for both approaches.

Enjoy! This book was created especially for your child's age group.
Talk about the story. Take turns reading favorite parts. Look at how
the illustrations support the story and enhance the reading experience.

And most of all, enjoy your child's journey into literacy. It's one of the
most important trips the two of you will ever take!

Whoosh! A family of bald eagles soars high. Did you know all of these birds almost disappeared? They were in danger of becoming extinct in parts of North America. Luckily, lots of people worked hard to protect the bald eagle. There are more bald eagles now than there were ten years ago. But other animals are still in danger!

The jaguar lives in the rain forest. It is a big, strong cat. Only the lion and the tiger are larger.

The jaguar has a spotted coat that makes this animal hard to see in its forest home. People like to wear jaguar fur. They think it is beautiful. Many jaguars have been killed for their coats.

Jaguars once lived as far north as Texas and New Mexico. Now they are found mostly in the rain forests of Central and South America. Even there, the jaguar is in danger. More and more of its home is being cut down.

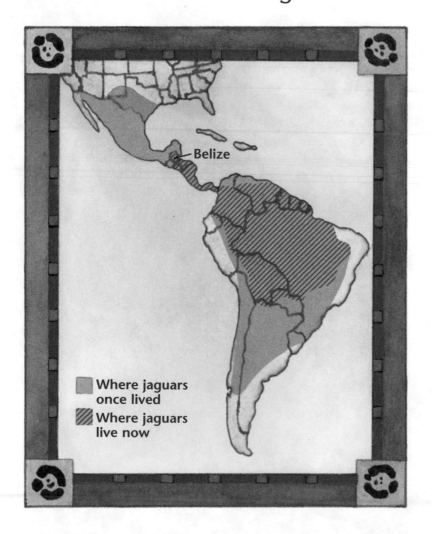

Belize

Where jaguars once lived

Where jaguars live now

Belize

Cockscomb Basin
Wildlife Sanctuary
and Jaguar Preserve

People in the small country of Belize
are doing something to save the
jaguar. They set aside a large piece
of land where jaguars are protected
and can roam freely. Belize has
made sure these big cats will not
disappear forever.

Gorillas look fierce, but they are actually quite shy and gentle. For many years, scientists thought that gorillas lived only in the lowlands of Africa. Then they discovered mountain gorillas in the African countries of Congo, Rwanda, and Uganda.

It didn't take long for illegal hunters, called poachers, to hear about this. They came with guns and hunted these gorillas until very few were left. Some poachers wanted to capture the gorillas to sell them to zoos. Others killed the mountain gorillas for their fur and for food.

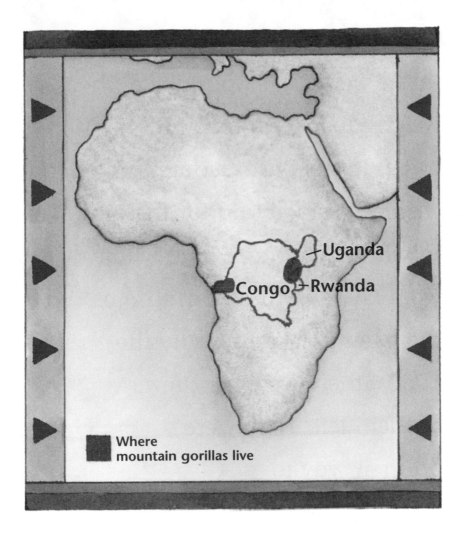

Where
mountain gorillas live

Many people spoke out against killing gorillas, and laws were passed to help protect them. The good news is that the mountain gorilla population is slowly increasing.

The blue whale is the largest animal in the world. A newborn blue whale weighs about two tons (1.8 metric tons)! In the past, people hunted whales for food and for the oil in whale fat. Many blue whales were killed at the beginning of the twentieth century. By the 1930s, there were very few of them left. They were on their way to becoming extinct.

Luckily, the blue whale has been saved by laws that limit hunting. Now there are over two thousand strong, healthy blue whales swimming off the coast of California. And more big babies are being born every year!

African elephants have big feet, big
ears, and big noses called trunks.
They also have large front teeth,
called tusks, that are made of ivory.

For many years people killed
elephants to take their tusks. They
wanted the ivory to carve into
jewelry and other handmade crafts.
Then, when very few African elephants
were left, a law was passed to stop
the hunting. But poachers still kill
elephants, because the ivory is worth
a lot of money.

JAGUAR

CROCODILE

MOUNTAIN GORILLA

BLUE WHALE

PANDA

AFRICAN ELEPHANT

ALASKAN GRIZZLY BEAR

BALD EAGLE

Today more and more people are
working to save the African elephant.
They are saying no to buying ivory.
They are saying yes to visiting Africa to
"shoot" elephants with their cameras!

Poachers aren't the only problem elephants face. People are moving onto their land. Elephants are vegetarians. They don't eat meat. They do eat more than five hundred pounds (225 kg) of plants each day! If large areas of grasslands disappear, elephants won't be able to find enough food. They could die off and become extinct.

Grizzly bears are very strong. One "grizz" can turn over a two-hundred-pound (90-kg) rock or knock down a small tree with a swipe of its paw.

The grizzly bear's strength has put it in danger. People are afraid of these animals and have hunted them for hundreds of years. Grizzly bears used to live in many parts of the United States, but now not many are left. They have survived by finding places where there are few humans. Today, the largest group of grizzly bears lives in Alaska. There is quite a lot of food for bears there, but there are only a small number of humans.

What will happen to grizzlies in the future? In Alaska, three safe areas have been set up for grizzly bears. No hunting is allowed there. In other states, people are trying to find open land where grizzly bears can live without becoming a danger to people. There are already small groups of grizzlies living in places such as Yellowstone National Park. We can hope that through these kinds of efforts, the grizzly bear will be with us for a long time.

Yellowstone
National Park

Wyoming

Alaska

Where grizzly
bears live

Giant pandas live in the mountains of China. They are in danger of dying out for two reasons. First, they are sometimes illegally hunted for their thick, beautiful black and white fur. Second, they eat mainly bamboo, which is a spiky plant with thick stalks. When the bamboo in one place is eaten or dies, the giant pandas must move on to other areas.

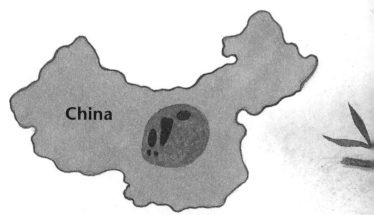

China

■ Where pandas live now

■ Where pandas once lived

Sometimes pandas can't move to find new feeding areas because people are in the way. Their farms block the path between one patch of bamboo and another. Giant pandas are very shy around humans and often will not cross their land.

Some people in China have created "panda corridors." These are paths of human-free land that connect one bamboo grove to another. The large, bearlike pandas follow these paths to find fresh sources of food. In this way, people are helping giant pandas survive.

Crocodiles are reptiles. They are part of the same family of animals as snakes, lizards, and turtles. Reptiles have been on Earth since the time of the dinosaurs! But now crocodiles are endangered. Why?

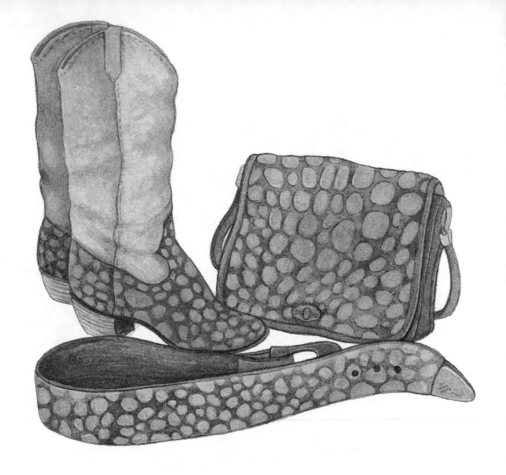

Between 1930 and 1960, a lot of crocodiles were killed for their skins. People made bags, belts, and shoes from the scaly, spotted, leathery skin of the crocodile. Laws were passed making it illegal to kill too many crocodiles. This helped, but today crocodiles still face problems.

Some people continue to kill them just for sport, or because they think the swamps where crocodiles live will be safer without these toothy creatures. Also, many swamps are becoming smaller and smaller. People drain them to make the land more usable, and when that happens, crocodiles lose their homes.

Some people are trying to make sure
that the crocodiles and their habitats
survive. One way they do this is through
a program called crocodile farming.
Crocodiles raised on farms are used to
supply meat and skins to consumers.
The crocodiles in the wild are left alone
to live in their natural environment.

There are many more animals in danger. We can help all of them by protecting their natural homes so they can live long lives, have lots of babies, and be part of our world for many years to come.

gray wolf

ocelot

spotted owl

sea turtle

whooping crane

bighorn sheep

Monito gecko

Index